FINANCIAL MASTERY

UNLOCKING THE SECRET TO WEALTH AND SUCCESS

JASON M. WOOD

All rights reserved. No part of this publication may be reproduced, distributed, or transmitted in any form or by any means, including photocopying, recording, or other electronic or mechanical methods, without the prior written permission of the publisher, except in the case of brief quotations embodied in critical reviews and certain other noncommercial uses permitted by copyright law.

Copyright © JASON M. WOOD, 2023.

Table of contents
Introduction
Chapter 1
Chapter 2
Chapter 3
Chapter 4
Chapter 5
Chapter 6
Chapter 7
Chapter 8
Conclusion

Introduction

Embark on a transformative journey towards financial mastery as you uncover the secrets to achieving lasting wealth and success. In this book, we guide you along a clear and purposeful path that leads to financial empowerment. You'll gain the essential knowledge, strategies, and mindset necessary to navigate the complexities of the financial world with confidence and clarity. Prepare to shift your perspective on money, learn practical tools for financial growth, and embark on a transformative journey that empowers you to create a life of abundance and fulfillment.

By following this path to financial mastery, you'll gain the knowledge and understanding needed to make informed decisions, overcome financial challenges, and unlock the doors to wealth and success. This path is not just about acquiring wealth, but also about developing a healthy relationship with money, cultivating a wealth mindset, and aligning your actions with your financial goals.

Throughout this book, we will explore various aspects of financial mastery, including personal finance, investing, building multiple streams of income, and overcoming obstacles along the way. Each chapter will provide you with valuable insights, practical strategies, and actionable steps to guide you on your journey.

The path to financial mastery is a lifelong endeavor, and this book serves as your trusted companion as you navigate its twists and turns. As you progress along this path, you'll gain confidence, develop resilience, and transform your financial reality. Prepare to unlock the secrets that will propel you towards lasting wealth and success, and embrace the power that comes from mastering your finances.

Remember, financial mastery is not solely about accumulating wealth; it's about gaining control over your financial destiny, creating a life of abundance, and having the freedom to pursue your passions. So, let's embark on this transformative journey together and discover the path to financial mastery that will empower you to live a life of prosperity and fulfillment.

Chapter 1

Mastering the Money Mindset

By mastering the money mindset, you can transform your beliefs, attitudes, and behaviors around money, allowing you to approach wealth creation with confidence and clarity. Here are key points to consider:

1. Shifting from Scarcity to Abundance: Embrace an abundance mindset that focuses on opportunities, possibilities, and gratitude. Release limiting beliefs about scarcity and lack, and instead cultivate an attitude of abundance, where you believe that there is enough wealth and prosperity for everyone.

2. Overcoming Money Blocks: Identify and address any subconscious money blocks that may be holding you back from achieving financial success. These blocks can include fear of failure, fear of success, guilt around wealth, or negative associations with money. By working through these blocks, you can remove barriers and create space for financial growth.

3. Developing Positive Money Habits: Cultivate healthy financial habits that support your goals and align with your desired outcomes. This includes practicing mindful spending, setting and following a budget, saving consistently, and investing wisely. By reinforcing positive money habits, you create a solid foundation for long-term financial success.

4. Visualizing and Affirming Financial Success: Utilize the power of visualization and affirmations to create a clear mental image of your financial goals and aspirations. Visualize yourself already achieving financial mastery, experiencing the lifestyle and abundance you desire. Use positive affirmations to reinforce your belief in your ability to create wealth and attract success.

5. Continual Growth and Learning:
Recognize that mastering the money mindset is an ongoing process. Commit to lifelong learning and personal growth in the realm of finance and wealth creation. Stay open to new ideas, strategies, and opportunities, and be willing to adapt and evolve as you progress on your financial journey.

By actively working on mastering your money mindset, you can transform your relationship with money, overcome limiting beliefs, and align your thoughts and actions with wealth creation. This sets the stage for unlocking the secrets to financial mastery and creating the wealth and success you desire.

Shifting Your Mindset for Financial Success
     Shifting your mindset is a powerful step towards achieving financial success. Your mindset shapes your thoughts, beliefs, and actions, ultimately influencing your financial

outcomes. Here's an explanation of how to shift your mindset for financial success:

1. Embrace a Growth Mindset: Adopt a growth mindset that believes in the potential for growth, learning, and improvement. Understand that your current financial situation does not define your future. Cultivate a belief that you can develop the skills, knowledge, and habits necessary for financial success.

2. Challenge Limiting Beliefs: Identify and challenge any limiting beliefs you may have about money, wealth, or your own capabilities. Common limiting beliefs include "money is scarce," "wealth is only for others," or "I'm not good with money." Replace these beliefs with empowering ones, such as "there are abundant opportunities to create wealth," "I deserve financial success," or "I can learn and improve my financial skills."

3. Focus on Possibilities and Solutions: Train your mind to focus on possibilities and solutions rather than dwelling on problems or limitations. Develop a problem-solving mindset that seeks creative ways to overcome financial challenges and find opportunities for growth. Cultivate optimism and resilience in the face of setbacks, viewing them as learning experiences and stepping stones towards success.

4. Surround Yourself with Positive Influences: Surround yourself with individuals who have a positive and success-oriented mindset. Seek out mentors, join communities or networks of like-minded individuals, and engage in conversations that inspire and motivate you. The people you surround yourself with can greatly impact your mindset and provide support on your financial journey.

5. Practice Gratitude and Abundance: Cultivate a sense of gratitude for what you currently have and the progress you've made. Shift your focus from what you lack to what you already possess. This mindset of abundance attracts more positive experiences and opportunities. Regularly express gratitude for your financial blessings and celebrate small wins along the way.

6. Visualize and Affirm Financial Success: Utilize the power of visualization and affirmations to reinforce your vision of financial success. Create vivid mental images of your desired financial outcomes and regularly visualize yourself already achieving those goals. Support these visualizations with positive affirmations that reinforce your belief in your ability to create wealth and abundance.

By shifting your mindset for financial success, you open yourself up to new possibilities, enhance your problem-solving abilities, and attract opportunities that align with your goals. With a growth mindset, empowering beliefs, and a focus on possibilities and solutions, you lay the foundation for a successful financial journey. Embrace the power of your mindset and watch as it propels you towards greater financial achievements.

Overcoming Limiting Beliefs about Money

Overcoming limiting beliefs about money is a crucial step towards achieving financial mastery. These beliefs can hold you back from making progress, taking risks, and pursuing opportunities that could lead to wealth and success. Here's an explanation of how to overcome limiting beliefs about money:

1. Identify Your Limiting Beliefs: Take the time to identify the specific limiting beliefs you hold about money. These can include beliefs such as "money is the root of all evil," "rich people are greedy," or "I'll never be able to earn a substantial income." Awareness is the first step towards challenging and changing these beliefs.

2. Challenge the Validity of Your Beliefs: Question the validity of your limiting beliefs and examine the evidence supporting or contradicting them. Seek alternative perspectives and examples of individuals who have achieved financial success while maintaining their integrity and making a positive impact. Understand that your beliefs are not facts, but rather interpretations and assumptions that can be changed.

3. Reframe Your Beliefs: Once you've identified and challenged your limiting beliefs, reframe them into more empowering and supportive beliefs. For example, "money is a tool for positive change and impact," "my financial success aligns with my values and purpose," or "I have the skills and abilities to create wealth and abundance." Reframing your beliefs opens up new possibilities and expands your mindset.

4. Replace Negative Self-Talk: Pay attention to your inner dialogue and replace negative self-talk with positive and empowering statements. Catch yourself when you engage in self-sabotaging thoughts like "I'm not good with money" or "I'll never be financially successful." Replace these statements with affirmations that reinforce your capabilities and potential for financial success.

5. Seek Evidence and Counterexamples: Look for evidence and counterexamples that contradict your limiting beliefs. Seek stories of individuals who have overcome similar beliefs and achieved financial success. Surround yourself with inspiring success stories, books, podcasts, or mentors who can provide alternative perspectives and reinforce your belief in what is possible.

6. Take Action and Prove Yourself Wrong: The most effective way to overcome limiting beliefs is to take action and prove yourself wrong. Start by setting small financial goals and working towards them. Celebrate your achievements along the way, and use them as evidence that challenges your old beliefs. As you experience progress, your newfound beliefs will become stronger and more rooted in reality.

By consciously working to overcome limiting beliefs about money, you free yourself from self-imposed constraints and open the door to greater financial possibilities. Remember that changing beliefs takes time and consistent effort. Stay committed to challenging and reframing your beliefs, surround yourself with positive influences, and take action towards your financial goals. Overcoming limiting beliefs will pave the way for true financial mastery and allow you to unlock the secrets to wealth and success.

Cultivating an Abundance Mentality
Cultivating an abundance mentality involves adopting a mindset that embraces the concept of abundance and wealth. It means shifting your focus from scarcity and lack to the belief that there are abundant opportunities and resources available to you. By cultivating an abundance

mentality, you open yourself up to attracting more wealth and success into your life.

Appreciating gratitude plays a crucial role in developing an abundance mentality. When you practice gratitude, you acknowledge and express gratitude for the things you already have, whether it's financial resources, relationships, or personal qualities. This practice shifts your focus towards the positive aspects of your life and helps you recognize the abundance that already exists.

To cultivate an abundance mentality, it's important to challenge and replace scarcity-based thoughts and beliefs with abundance-focused ones. Instead of dwelling on what you lack, focus on what you have and what is possible. By shifting your mindset from scarcity to abundance, you create a positive outlook that attracts more opportunities for wealth and success.

Believing in abundance and possibility is another key aspect of cultivating an abundance mentality. It involves developing a deep-seated belief that abundance is your natural state and that opportunities for financial success are available to you. By embracing this belief, you align your thoughts and actions with the abundance you desire, increasing your chances of achieving it.

Practicing generosity is an effective way to cultivate an abundance mentality. By sharing your wealth, time, and resources with others, you demonstrate your belief in the abundance of resources available. This practice creates a positive flow of abundance in your life and reinforces the mindset of abundance.

Surrounding yourself with individuals who already have an abundance mentality can greatly influence your own mindset. Engage in conversations, join communities, or seek mentors who have a positive outlook on wealth and success. Their mindset and energy will support and inspire your own abundance mentality.

Cultivating an abundance mentality also requires taking action and seizing opportunities. It's not enough to have a positive mindset; you must also be proactive in seeking out avenues for financial growth and wealth creation. Embrace calculated risks, step out of your comfort zone, and be open to exploring new possibilities.

By cultivating an abundance mentality, you shift your mindset towards abundance and attract more opportunities for financial success into your life. Embrace gratitude, challenge scarcity thinking, surround yourself with abundance-minded individuals, and take action towards your goals. Cultivating an abundance mentality is an essential step towards unlocking the secrets to financial mastery and achieving lasting wealth and success.

Chapter 2

Building a Solid Financial Foundation

Building a solid financial foundation is crucial for long-term financial success and stability. It involves establishing healthy financial habits, setting clear goals, and making wise decisions that lay the groundwork for a strong financial future. Here's an explanation of how to build a solid financial foundation:

1. Establish a Budget: Creating a budget is a fundamental step in building a solid financial foundation. It involves tracking your income and expenses, allocating funds for essential needs, savings, and investments, and ensuring that you live within your means. A budget provides a clear roadmap for managing your finances effectively.

2. Save and Invest Regularly: Saving and investing are essential components of building wealth and financial security. Set aside a portion of your income each month for savings and investments. Start an emergency fund to cover unexpected expenses and establish long-term investment strategies to grow your wealth over time. Consistency is key in building a strong financial foundation.

3. Manage Debt Wisely: Debt can be a significant obstacle to financial stability. To build a solid financial foundation, focus on managing your debt wisely. Minimize high-interest debt, such as credit card debt, and prioritize paying it off as soon as possible. Create a repayment plan and make consistent payments to reduce your debt burden.

4. Establish an Emergency Fund: An emergency fund acts as a financial safety net. Aim to save three to six months' worth of living expenses in an easily accessible account. This fund will provide a buffer during unexpected events like job loss, medical emergencies, or major repairs, ensuring that you can handle financial challenges without derailing your progress.

5. Protect Yourself with Insurance: Insurance plays a vital role in building a solid financial foundation. Evaluate your insurance needs, including health insurance, life insurance, property insurance, and disability insurance. Adequate coverage protects you and your loved ones from significant financial risks and provides peace of mind.

6. Set Financial Goals: Clearly define your financial goals to guide your actions and decisions. Whether it's buying a home, starting a business, or retiring comfortably, having specific goals helps you stay focused and motivated. Break down your goals into smaller, actionable steps and regularly review your progress to make necessary adjustments.

7. Educate Yourself: Take the time to educate yourself about personal finance and investment strategies. Stay informed about financial trends, learn about different investment options, and seek guidance from financial experts if needed. Knowledge empowers you to make informed decisions and navigate the financial landscape effectively.

8. Review and Adjust Regularly: Building a solid financial foundation is an ongoing process. Regularly review your financial situation, track your progress towards goals, and make necessary adjustments along the way. Life circumstances and financial markets change, so staying adaptable and proactive ensures that your foundation remains strong.

By building a solid financial foundation, you establish a framework for long-term financial success. A budget, savings, wise debt management, emergency funds, insurance, clear goals, continuous education, and regular review are all essential elements. With a solid foundation, you can weather financial challenges, seize opportunities, and achieve your desired level of financial security and prosperity.

Creating a Budget that Works for You

Creating a budget that works for you is a vital step in managing your finances effectively and building a solid financial foundation. A well-planned budget allows you to allocate your income wisely, prioritize your spending, and make informed financial decisions. Here's an explanation of how to create a budget that works for you:

1. Assess Your Income: Start by assessing your income sources, including your salary, freelance work, investments, or any other sources of income. Calculate your total monthly income based on these sources.

2. Track Your Expenses: Track your expenses for a designated period, such as a month, to gain a clear understanding of where your money is going. Categorize your expenses into different categories such as housing, transportation, groceries, entertainment, and so on. This step helps you identify areas where you may be overspending or can potentially cut back.

3. Differentiate Between Needs and Wants: Differentiate between your needs and wants to prioritize your spending. Needs include essential expenses like rent/mortgage, utilities, groceries, transportation, and healthcare. Wants are discretionary expenses like dining out, entertainment, travel, and non-essential shopping. By distinguishing between the two, you can allocate your funds accordingly.

4. Set Financial Goals: Determine your short-term and long-term financial goals. These may include saving for a down payment on a house, paying off debt, creating an emergency fund, or planning for retirement. Your budget should align with these goals and allocate funds towards achieving them.

5. Allocate Income to Categories: Allocate your income to the different expense categories based on your needs, wants, and financial goals. Start by covering your essential expenses and savings/investment goals. Then, distribute the remaining income among discretionary expenses while keeping in mind your financial priorities.

6. Track and Monitor Your Budget: Regularly track and monitor your budget to ensure you're staying within your allocated amounts for each category. Use budgeting tools, spreadsheets, or mobile apps to help you keep track of your income and expenses. Review your budget periodically and make adjustments as needed to accommodate any changes in income or expenses.

7. Find Areas to Cut Back: Analyze your spending patterns to identify areas where you can cut back and save money. Look for subscriptions or services you no longer need, find ways to reduce utility bills, or explore cost-effective alternatives for entertainment or dining out. Redirect the saved funds towards your financial goals or other priority areas.

8. Be Flexible and Adjust as Needed:
Recognize that your budget may need adjustments over time. Life circumstances, income fluctuations, or changing financial goals may require you to modify your budget. Stay flexible and make necessary adjustments to ensure your budget continues to work effectively for your current situation.

By creating a budget that works for you, you gain control over your finances and make intentional decisions about how you allocate your income. Assess your income, track expenses, differentiate between needs and wants, set financial goals, allocate income to categories, track and monitor your budget, find areas to cut back, and be flexible in making adjustments. A well-designed budget empowers you to make progress towards your financial goals and paves the way for a solid financial foundation.

Tackling Debt and Managing Credit

Tackling debt and managing credit are essential aspects of achieving financial mastery and building a solid financial foundation. Here's an explanation of how to effectively tackle debt and manage credit:

1. Assess Your Debt: Start by assessing your current debt situation. Make a list of all your outstanding debts, including credit cards, student loans, personal loans, and any other forms of debt. Note down the total amount owed, interest rates, minimum payments, and due dates for each debt.

2. Create a Repayment Strategy: Develop a repayment strategy to tackle your debts systematically. Consider two common approaches: the "Debt Snowball" and the "Debt Avalanche." With the Debt Snowball method, focus on paying off the smallest debt first while making minimum payments on other debts.

Once the smallest debt is paid off, apply that payment amount to the next smallest debt. The Debt Avalanche method involves prioritizing debts with the highest interest rates, paying them off first while making minimum payments on other debts. Choose the strategy that aligns best with your financial circumstances and personal preference.

3. Reduce Expenses and Increase Income: To accelerate debt repayment, look for ways to reduce expenses and increase your income. Analyze your budget to identify areas where you can cut back on discretionary spending and redirect those funds towards debt repayment. Additionally, consider ways to increase your income, such as taking on a side gig, freelancing, or seeking a raise at work. The extra income can be applied towards debt reduction.

4. Negotiate with Creditors: If you're struggling to meet your debt obligations, consider negotiating with your creditors. Reach out to them to discuss options such as reduced interest rates, extended payment terms, or debt settlement arrangements. Many creditors are willing to work with you to find mutually beneficial solutions.

5. Avoid Taking on New Debt: While focusing on debt repayment, avoid taking on new debt. Minimize the use of credit cards and be cautious about new loan applications. Instead, focus on living within your means and using cash or debit for purchases. This approach prevents further accumulation of debt and allows you to make progress in reducing existing debt.

6. Build a Positive Credit History: While managing your debt, it's important to build and maintain a positive credit history. Pay all your bills on time and in full, as this helps establish a good credit score. Monitor your credit reports regularly to ensure accuracy and address any errors promptly. A strong credit history can benefit you in future endeavors, such as obtaining favorable loan terms or securing lower insurance rates.

7. Seek Professional Assistance if Needed: If you're overwhelmed with debt or struggling to manage your finances effectively, consider seeking professional assistance. Credit counseling agencies or financial advisors can provide guidance and support tailored to your specific situation. They can help you develop a personalized debt management plan and provide valuable insights into improving your financial well-being.

By tackling debt and managing credit effectively, you take control of your financial situation and pave the way towards financial freedom. Assess your debt, create a repayment strategy, reduce expenses and increase income, negotiate with creditors, avoid new debt, build a positive credit history, and seek professional assistance when necessary. These steps will help you regain control over your finances and work towards a debt-free and financially secure future.

Establishing an Emergency Fund

An emergency fund is a dedicated savings account specifically designed to cover unexpected expenses or financial emergencies. Here's a detailed explanation of how to establish an emergency fund:

1. Recognize the Importance of an Emergency Fund: Understand the significance of having an emergency fund as a cornerstone of your financial well-being. An emergency fund serves as a financial safety net, providing a cushion to protect you from unexpected events such as medical emergencies, job loss, major home repairs, or car breakdowns. It ensures that you can address these situations without resorting to high-interest debt or jeopardizing your long-term financial goals.

2. Determine Your Target Emergency Fund Amount: Assess your financial situation and determine how much you need to save in your emergency fund. Aim to save three to six months' worth of living expenses, although the exact amount may vary depending on individual circumstances. Consider factors such as your income stability, job security, dependents, and specific financial obligations. The goal is to have enough funds to cover essential expenses during an extended period of financial uncertainty.

3. Set a Realistic Saving Goal: Break down your target emergency fund amount into manageable saving goals. Determine a specific monthly or weekly saving target that aligns with your income and expenses. Automate regular contributions to your emergency fund to ensure consistent progress. Start with an achievable amount and gradually increase your contributions as you free up more funds or receive extra income.

4. Prioritize Building Your Emergency Fund: Make saving for your emergency fund a priority in your overall financial plan. Treat it as an essential expense that must be met every month, just like your rent or mortgage payment. Cut back on non-essential expenses or find ways to increase your income to allocate more funds toward your emergency savings.

5. Choose the Right Account: Select a suitable savings account for your emergency fund. Look for an account that offers high liquidity and easy access to your funds when needed. Consider options like a traditional savings account, a money market account, or a dedicated emergency fund account. Compare interest rates and fees to maximize the growth of your savings while maintaining accessibility.

6. Protect Your Emergency Fund: Safeguard your emergency fund from being used for non-emergency purposes. Resist the temptation to dip into it for discretionary expenses or impulse purchases. Separate your emergency fund from your regular spending accounts to maintain its purpose and integrity. Maintain discipline and a long-term perspective when it comes to your emergency savings.

7. Replenish and Reevaluate: If you ever need to use your emergency fund, make replenishing it a priority once the financial crisis has passed. Adjust your saving goals accordingly and aim to restore your emergency fund to its target amount as soon as possible. Additionally, periodically reassess your target amount and adjust it based on changes in your financial circumstances.

By establishing an emergency fund, you create a strong financial foundation that enhances your overall financial security and success. Recognize its importance, determine your target amount, set realistic saving goals, prioritize saving, choose the right account, protect your funds, and replenish as needed. An emergency fund gives you peace of mind and the confidence to navigate unexpected financial challenges, allowing you to focus on achieving long-term wealth and success.

Chapter 3

The Power of Saving and Investing

Understanding the immense potential of saving and investing is key to achieving financial mastery and unlocking the secrets to wealth and success.

Saving:

Saving is a fundamental aspect of financial management that involves setting aside a portion of your income for future use instead of spending it all immediately. Saving provides a solid financial foundation by creating a safety net for unexpected expenses, allowing you to pursue short-term goals, and instilling disciplined financial habits. By prioritizing saving, you take control of your finances, avoid excessive debt, and establish a strong base for long-term growth and prosperity.

Investing:

Investing takes saving to the next level by putting your money to work to generate potential returns. Through investing, you allocate your saved funds into various investment vehicles such as stocks, bonds, mutual funds, real estate, or other assets. Investing allows your money to grow over time, leveraging the power of compounding. By earning returns on your initial investment and reinvesting those returns, your wealth can multiply exponentially.

The Benefits:
The power of saving and investing lies in the numerous benefits they offer:

1. Wealth Accumulation: Saving and investing provide opportunities for long-term wealth accumulation. By consistently setting aside funds and intelligently investing them, you can grow your net worth over time. This accumulation of wealth can lead to financial freedom, opportunities for personal growth, and the ability to achieve your desired lifestyle.

2. Financial Security: Saving and investing help you build a financial safety net. By having savings and investments, you can weather unexpected emergencies, navigate economic downturns, and maintain financial stability. This security allows you to face challenges with confidence and peace of mind.

3. Passive Income: Investing in income-generating assets such as stocks that pay dividends or rental properties can provide you with passive income streams. Passive income is money earned without actively working for it, and it can provide financial freedom and flexibility.

4. Retirement Planning: Saving and investing are vital for retirement planning. By consistently contributing to retirement accounts, such as a 401(k) or individual retirement account (IRA), you can ensure a comfortable and secure retirement. Investing these funds wisely allows you to benefit from long-term growth potential and enjoy a fulfilling post-work life.

5. Achieving Financial Goals: Saving and investing enable you to achieve your financial goals. Whether it's purchasing a home, funding education, starting a business, or traveling the world, having savings and strategically investing can help you realize your dreams and aspirations.

In summary, the power of saving and investing lies in their ability to build financial security, accumulate wealth, generate passive income, plan for retirement, and achieve your financial goals. By understanding and harnessing this power, you can unlock the secrets to wealth and success, ultimately attaining financial mastery.

Understanding the Importance of Saving

Saving plays a critical role in financial mastery and uncovering the keys to wealth and success. Here's an explanation of why saving is crucial:

1. Financial Security: Saving provides a safety net and financial stability. It ensures that you have funds available for unexpected expenses, emergencies, and challenging times. By having savings, you can avoid relying on credit or incurring debt, giving you peace of mind and a solid foundation for your financial well-being.

2. Future Planning: Saving allows you to plan for your future and achieve your financial goals. Whether it's buying a home, starting a business, or securing your retirement, saving regularly enables you to accumulate the necessary funds to turn your aspirations into reality. It empowers you to take control of your financial destiny and shape the life you desire.

3. Emergency Preparedness: Life is unpredictable, and unforeseen expenses can arise at any time. By saving, you create an emergency fund that serves as a financial safety net. This fund provides a buffer to handle unexpected situations such as medical bills, car repairs, or job loss, allowing you to navigate these challenges without jeopardizing your financial stability.

4. Debt Management: Saving plays a vital role in managing and minimizing debt. By having savings, you can cover expenses without resorting to loans or credit cards. This helps you avoid the burden of high-interest debt and prevents it from becoming a hindrance to your financial progress. Saving empowers you to maintain control over your finances and work towards a debt-free future.

5. Financial Independence: Saving fosters financial independence by giving you greater control over your money and choices. It liberates you from living paycheck to paycheck and allows you to make decisions based on your values and long-term goals. With savings, you have the freedom to pursue opportunities, invest in your personal growth, and create a more secure and fulfilling financial future.

6. Wealth Creation: Saving is the foundation for building wealth. It provides the capital needed to invest in income-generating assets and opportunities. By saving consistently and investing wisely, you can leverage the power of compounding and grow your wealth over time. Saving facilitates the creation of passive income streams and paves the way for long-term financial prosperity.

In summary, understanding the importance of saving is paramount on the path to financial mastery. Saving brings financial security, empowers future planning, prepares you for emergencies, aids in debt management, promotes financial independence, and serves as a catalyst for wealth creation. By embracing the significance of saving, you unlock the doors to wealth and success, and pave the way for a prosperous financial journey.

Introduction to Different Investment Vehicles

Different investment vehicles offer unique opportunities for wealth creation and financial success. Here are some key investment options to consider:

1. Stocks: Stocks represent ownership in a company and can provide significant returns over time. Investing in stocks allows you to participate in the company's growth and potentially earn dividends.

2. Bonds: Bonds are debt instruments issued by governments or corporations. By investing in bonds, you lend money and receive interest payments over a specified period.

3. Mutual Funds: Mutual funds pool money from multiple investors to invest in a diversified portfolio of stocks, bonds, or other securities. They offer professional management and diversification.

4. Exchange-Traded Funds (ETFs): ETFs are similar to mutual funds but trade on stock exchanges like individual stocks. They provide exposure to specific sectors or indexes.

5. Real Estate: Investing in real estate involves purchasing properties for rental income or appreciation. Real estate can provide both cash flow and long-term value growth.

6. Commodities: Commodities include tangible goods like gold, oil, or agricultural products. Investing in commodities can serve as a hedge against inflation or a way to diversify your portfolio.

7. Cryptocurrencies: Cryptocurrencies like Bitcoin and Ethereum have gained popularity as digital assets. They offer potential high returns but also come with higher risks due to their volatility.

Understanding the characteristics and potential risks of each investment vehicle is crucial for making informed investment decisions. By diversifying your investments across different asset classes, you can potentially mitigate risks and maximize returns on your path to financial mastery and wealth accumulation.

Developing a Long-Term Investment Strategy

A well-defined long-term investment strategy is key to achieving financial mastery and unlocking the secrets to wealth and success. Here are steps on how to develop an effective long-term investment strategy:

1. Set Clear Financial Goals: Start by defining your financial goals. Identify what you want to achieve in the long term, such as retirement planning, funding your children's education, or purchasing a property. Setting clear goals helps you align your investment strategy with your aspirations.

2. Assess Your Risk Tolerance: Understand your risk tolerance, which is your ability and willingness to endure market fluctuations. Consider factors such as your age, time horizon, financial obligations, and comfort level with volatility. This assessment will guide your investment decisions and asset allocation.

3. Diversify Your Portfolio: Diversification is crucial for long-term investing. Spread your investments across different asset classes, such as stocks, bonds, real estate, and commodities. Diversification helps reduce risk and ensures that potential losses in one area can be offset by gains in others.

4. Consider Time in the Market: Time in the market is more important than timing the market. Instead of trying to predict short-term market movements, focus on staying invested for the long term. Historically, long-term investing has generated more consistent returns and helped investors weather market volatility.

5. Choose Appropriate Investment Vehicles: Select investment vehicles that align with your financial goals and risk tolerance. For example, if you have a longer time horizon and can handle higher risk, investing in stocks or equity-based funds may be suitable. If you prefer stability and income, consider fixed-income investments like bonds or dividend-paying stocks.

6. Regularly Monitor and Rebalance: Keep track of your investments and review their performance periodically. Rebalance your portfolio as needed to maintain your desired asset allocation. Adjustments may be necessary to align with changes in your financial goals or market conditions.

7. Seek Professional Guidance: Consider consulting with a financial advisor or investment professional to help you develop and fine-tune your long-term investment strategy. They can provide expertise, objective advice, and help navigate complex investment decisions.

Remember, developing a long-term investment strategy requires patience, discipline, and ongoing evaluation. Regularly assess your progress towards your financial goals and make adjustments as necessary. By following a well-designed long-term investment strategy, you enhance your chances of achieving financial mastery and realizing your dreams of wealth and success.

Chapter 4

Growing Your Wealth through Strategic Investing

Growing your wealth through strategic investing is an effective way to build financial security and achieve long-term goals. Here are some key steps and considerations to keep in mind:

1. Set Clear Financial Goals: Start by defining your financial objectives. Do you want to save for retirement, buy a house, fund your children's education, or achieve financial independence? Clear goals will help guide your investment decisions.

2. Assess Risk Tolerance: Determine your risk tolerance, which reflects your ability and willingness to withstand potential investment losses. Younger individuals with a longer time horizon can typically tolerate more risk, while those nearing retirement may prefer more conservative investments.

3. Diversify Your Portfolio: Diversification is essential for managing risk. Allocate your investment capital across different asset classes, such as stocks, bonds, real estate, and commodities. Within each asset class, diversify further by investing in different industries or geographic regions.

4. Educate Yourself: Take the time to learn about different investment options, understand how markets work, and stay updated on economic trends. Read books, attend seminars, follow financial news, and consider consulting with a financial advisor to gain knowledge and make informed decisions.

5. Create a Long-Term Investment Strategy: Develop a well-thought-out investment strategy based on your goals, risk tolerance, and time horizon. Decide whether you want to be an active investor, managing your portfolio regularly, or a passive investor, utilizing low-cost index funds or exchange-traded funds (ETFs).

6. Invest in Quality Assets: Focus on investments with a proven track record of generating solid returns over time. Look for assets that have a competitive advantage, strong management teams, and sustainable business models. Conduct thorough research and analysis before investing in individual stocks or bonds.

7. Consider Dollar-Cost Averaging: This strategy involves regularly investing a fixed amount of money at regular intervals, regardless of market conditions. By doing so, you can potentially buy more shares when prices are low and fewer shares when prices are high, reducing the impact of short-term market volatility.

8. Monitor and Rebalance: Regularly review your investment portfolio to ensure it aligns with your goals and risk tolerance. Rebalance your holdings periodically to maintain your desired asset allocation. This involves selling some investments that have performed well and buying more of those that have underperformed to maintain your desired asset allocation.

9. Stay Disciplined and Avoid Emotional Decisions: Emotional investing can lead to costly mistakes. Stick to your long-term investment strategy and avoid making impulsive decisions based on short-term market fluctuations. Remember that investing is a long-term endeavor, and patience is key.

10. Seek Professional Advice if Needed: If you feel overwhelmed or lack the expertise and time to manage your investments, consider working with a qualified financial advisor who can provide personalized guidance based on your individual circumstances.

Remember, investing involves risk, and there are no guarantees of returns. It's crucial to do your due diligence, stay informed, and make investment decisions based on your own research and financial situation.

Diving Deeper into Stocks, Bonds, and Mutual Funds

Certainly! Let's dive deeper into stocks, bonds, and mutual funds—the three commonly used investment vehicles:

1. Stocks:

  - Stocks represent ownership in a company. When you buy shares of a company's stock, you become a partial owner, entitled to a portion of its profits and assets.

  - Stocks offer potential capital appreciation (increasing value over time) and may provide dividends (a portion of the company's profits distributed to shareholders).

  - They can be classified into different categories, such as common stocks (basic ownership shares) and preferred stocks (with specific privileges but limited voting rights).

- Investing in stocks carries higher risk compared to bonds, but it also offers the potential for higher returns.

- It's essential to research and analyze individual companies before investing in their stocks, considering factors such as financial performance, management team, competitive advantages, and industry trends.

2. Bonds:

- Bonds are debt securities issued by governments, municipalities, or corporations to raise capital. When you buy a bond, you are effectively lending money to the issuer in exchange for regular interest payments and the return of the principal at maturity.

- Bonds are generally considered less risky than stocks because they offer fixed interest payments and the return of principal, assuming the issuer doesn't default.

- They come in different types, including government bonds, municipal bonds, corporate bonds, and treasury bonds. Each type carries varying levels of risk and potential returns.

- Bond prices are influenced by interest rates and credit ratings. When interest rates rise, bond prices typically fall, and vice versa.
- Investors who seek stable income and capital preservation often include bonds in their portfolios.

3. Mutual Funds:
- Mutual funds pool money from multiple investors to invest in a diversified portfolio of stocks, bonds, or other assets, managed by professional fund managers.
- They offer investors the opportunity to access a diversified investment portfolio with a relatively small investment.
- Mutual funds come in various types, such as equity funds (investing in stocks), bond funds (investing in bonds), balanced funds (investing in both stocks and bonds), index funds (tracking a specific market index), and sector-specific funds (focusing on specific industries or sectors).
- Mutual funds can be actively managed (where fund managers aim to outperform the

market) or passively managed (aiming to match the performance of a specific index).

- Investors in mutual funds typically pay fees and expenses, including management fees and operating expenses.

It's important to note that the performance of stocks, bonds, and mutual funds can be influenced by various factors, including economic conditions, market volatility, interest rates, and geopolitical events. Additionally, past performance is not indicative of future results.

Before investing in any of these options, it's advisable to conduct thorough research, assess your risk tolerance, and consider consulting with a financial advisor to determine the most suitable investment approach for your financial goals and circumstances.

Exploring Real Estate and Alternative Investments

Real estate and alternative investments can offer diversification and unique opportunities for investors. Here's an overview of these investment options:

1. Real Estate:

- Real estate investments involve purchasing properties or investing in real estate-related assets.
- Residential properties, commercial properties (such as office buildings, retail spaces), industrial properties, and real estate investment trusts (REITs) are common avenues for real estate investment.
- Benefits of real estate investments include potential appreciation in property value, rental income, tax advantages (e.g., mortgage interest deductions), and a hedge against inflation.
- Real estate investments require careful consideration of factors such as location, property condition, rental demand, financing

options, property management, and market trends.

- Investors can choose to be directly involved in property ownership or invest in real estate funds or REITs, which offer exposure to a diversified portfolio of properties.

2. Alternative Investments:

- Alternative investments are non-traditional asset classes beyond stocks, bonds, and cash.
- These investments have a relatively low correlation with traditional assets and can provide diversification benefits to a portfolio.
- Examples of alternative investments include:
  - Hedge funds: Private investment funds that aim to generate positive returns regardless of market conditions, often using complex investment strategies.
  - Private Equity: Investing in privately held companies or buying stakes in existing businesses with the aim of improving performance and selling at a profit.
  - Venture Capital: Investing in early-stage companies with high growth potential.

- Commodities: Investing in physical goods like gold, oil, or agricultural products.

- Art, collectibles, and fine wines: Investing in tangible assets that can appreciate in value over time.

- Peer-to-peer lending: Participating in online platforms that connect borrowers with lenders, providing opportunities for fixed-income returns.

- Alternative investments typically have different risk profiles and may have limited liquidity or require longer investment horizons.

- Due diligence, understanding the underlying assets or strategies, and assessing the track record of fund managers are crucial when investing in alternatives.

It's important to note that real estate and alternative investments can involve complex legal, financial, and regulatory considerations. It's recommended to consult with professionals, such as real estate agents, financial advisors, or legal experts, to ensure you have a thorough understanding of the risks and opportunities associated with these investments. Additionally, each investment option may have specific tax implications, so it's wise to consult with a tax advisor to understand the tax aspects of these investments as well.

Mitigating Risks and Maximizing Returns
Mitigating risks and maximizing returns are crucial aspects of investment management. While no investment is completely risk-free, there are strategies you can employ to manage risks and aim for better returns. Here are some key considerations:

1. Diversification: Diversifying your investment portfolio is a fundamental risk management strategy. Allocate your investments across different asset classes (e.g., stocks, bonds, real estate) and within each asset class (e.g., different industries, regions). Diversification can help reduce the impact of volatility in any single investment and potentially enhance overall returns.

2. Risk Assessment: Understand and assess the risks associated with each investment. Consider factors such as market volatility, economic conditions, interest rate changes, geopolitical events, and specific risks associated with the investment type (e.g., credit risk for bonds, tenant vacancy risk for real estate). Evaluate your risk tolerance and align your investments accordingly.

3. Asset Allocation: Develop an appropriate asset allocation strategy based on your investment goals, risk tolerance, and time horizon. Asset allocation involves deciding how much of your portfolio to allocate to different asset classes. It's a balancing act that aims to optimize returns while managing risks. Regularly review and rebalance your portfolio to maintain your desired asset allocation.

4. Research and Due Diligence: Thoroughly research and analyze investment opportunities before committing capital. Understand the fundamentals of the investments, including financial performance, management quality, competitive positioning, and growth potential. Consider both qualitative and quantitative factors to make informed investment decisions.

5. Dollar-Cost Averaging: Implementing a dollar-cost averaging strategy can help mitigate the impact of market volatility. By investing a fixed amount at regular intervals, you buy more shares when prices are low and fewer shares when prices are high. Over time, this strategy can potentially result in a lower average cost per share and mitigate the risks associated with market timing.

6. Regular Monitoring and Review: Continuously monitor your investments and stay updated on market trends and economic developments. Regularly review your portfolio's performance and make adjustments as needed. However, avoid making impulsive decisions based solely on short-term market fluctuations.

Focus on the long-term goals of your investment strategy.

7. Consider Professional Advice: If you are uncertain about managing your investments or lack the time and expertise, consider consulting with a qualified financial advisor. They can provide personalized guidance, help assess risks, identify suitable investment opportunities, and offer strategies to maximize returns based on your specific financial situation and goals.

8. Stay Informed and Educated: Keep learning about investment strategies, economic trends, and financial markets. Read books, follow reputable financial news sources, and consider attending investment seminars or webinars. Being well-informed can help you make better investment decisions.

Remember, investing involves risks, and there are no guarantees of returns. It's essential to carefully consider your financial goals, risk tolerance, and investment horizon when implementing strategies to mitigate risks and maximize returns.

Chapter 5

Generating Passive Income Streams

Generating passive income streams is a great way to build financial stability and achieve financial independence. Passive income refers to earnings that are generated with minimal ongoing effort or active involvement. Here are some popular passive income streams:

1. Rental Properties: Owning and renting out real estate properties can provide steady rental income. This could include residential properties, commercial spaces, vacation rentals, or even renting out a portion of your own home.

2. Dividend Stocks: Investing in dividend-paying stocks allows you to earn regular income through dividend distributions. Dividend stocks are shares of companies that distribute a portion of their profits to shareholders.

3. Peer-to-Peer Lending: Participating in peer-to-peer lending platforms enables you to lend money to individuals or small businesses in exchange for interest payments. This can be done through online platforms that connect borrowers and lenders.

4. Royalties: If you own intellectual property, such as patents, copyrights, or trademarks, you can earn royalties from licensing or allowing others to use your intellectual property.

5. Digital Products: Creating and selling digital products, such as e-books, online courses, stock photos, or software applications, can generate passive income once the initial work is done.

6. Affiliate Marketing: Promoting other people's products or services through affiliate marketing programs can earn you commissions for every sale or lead generated through your referral.

7. Real Estate Investment Trusts (REITs): Investing in REITs allows you to become a partial owner of a portfolio of income-generating real estate properties. REITs are publicly traded companies that own, operate, or finance income-generating real estate.

8. High-Yield Savings Accounts and Certificates of Deposit (CDs): While not as lucrative as other options, placing funds in high-yield savings accounts or CDs can provide a low-risk way to earn passive income through interest.

9. Online Advertising: If you have a website or blog with significant traffic, you can monetize it through online advertising platforms, such as Google AdSense, and earn passive income from ad impressions or clicks.

10. Rental Income from Assets: Besides real estate, you can also earn rental income from other assets like vehicles, equipment, or storage spaces.

It's important to note that some passive income streams may require initial effort and ongoing maintenance, especially during the setup phase. Additionally, passive income should not be seen as completely hands-off, as periodic monitoring and adjustments may be necessary.

Remember to do thorough research, assess the risks and potential returns, and consult with professionals if needed, to ensure that your passive income endeavors align with your financial goals and risk tolerance.

Unleashing the Potential of Passive Income
Passive income has the potential to provide financial freedom and flexibility. To unleash its full potential, consider the following strategies:

1. Build Multiple Streams: Diversify your passive income sources to reduce reliance on a single stream. By having multiple income streams, you create a more resilient and balanced portfolio of passive income sources.

2. Optimize Existing Streams: Continuously evaluate and optimize your existing passive income streams to maximize their potential. For example, with rental properties, consider increasing rents periodically, improving property management efficiency, or exploring short-term rentals.

3. Leverage Technology: Embrace technology to scale your passive income efforts. Leverage automation tools, online platforms, and digital marketing techniques to streamline processes, reach a broader audience, and increase efficiency.

4. Create Evergreen Content: When creating digital products or content for online platforms, focus on evergreen content—content that remains relevant and valuable over time. This ensures a continuous stream of income without the need for constant updates.

5. Grow Your Network: Networking can open doors to new passive income opportunities. Attend industry events, connect with like-minded individuals, join relevant communities, and explore partnerships or joint ventures that align with your passive income goals.

6. Continual Learning and Skill Development: Invest in acquiring new skills or enhancing existing ones that can contribute to your passive income pursuits. This could involve learning about digital marketing, investment analysis, content creation, or any other relevant skills that align with your chosen streams.

7. Scale Up Successful Ventures: Once you identify a successful passive income stream, explore ways to scale it up. This could involve expanding your rental property portfolio, increasing advertising efforts for your online business, or creating additional digital products within the same niche.

8. Reinvest and Compound: Consider reinvesting a portion of your passive income back into your ventures to accelerate growth. Reinvesting earnings can help you expand your portfolio, increase marketing efforts, or develop new products, thereby compounding your passive income potential.

9. Stay Adaptive and Open to New Opportunities: The world is constantly evolving, and new passive income opportunities emerge. Stay adaptable and open to exploring new ideas, industries, and technologies that align with your interests and skills.

10. Monitor and Review: Regularly monitor the performance of your passive income streams and make adjustments as needed. Stay informed about market trends, industry developments, and changes in regulations that may impact your income sources.

Remember, building a sustainable and profitable passive income portfolio takes time, effort, and continuous evaluation. Be patient, persistent, and willing to learn from both successes and setbacks along the way.

Exploring Rental Properties and Real Estate Investments

Rental properties and real estate investments can be attractive options for generating passive income and building wealth over time. Here's a closer look at these investment avenues:

1. Rental Properties:
- Rental properties involve purchasing residential or commercial properties and renting them out to tenants.
- Residential properties include single-family homes, apartments, condominiums, or

townhouses. Commercial properties encompass office buildings, retail spaces, warehouses, or industrial properties.

- Benefits of rental properties include regular rental income, potential property value appreciation, tax advantages (e.g., deductions for mortgage interest and property expenses), and potential leverage through financing.

- Key considerations include property location, market demand, property management (self-managed or hiring a property management company), tenant screening, maintenance costs, and local landlord-tenant laws and regulations.

- Conducting thorough market research, analyzing rental income potential, and evaluating the financial feasibility (including costs, financing options, and potential returns) are essential steps before investing in rental properties.

2. Real Estate Investment Trusts (REITs):

- REITs are publicly traded companies that own, operate, or finance income-generating real estate properties.

- By investing in REITs, individuals can gain exposure to a diversified portfolio of real estate assets without directly owning properties.
- REITs typically focus on specific property types (e.g., residential, commercial, healthcare, or industrial) or investment strategies (e.g., development, income generation, or mortgage financing).
- Investors in REITs earn dividends from the rental income generated by the underlying properties.
- REITs provide liquidity, as their shares can be bought and sold on stock exchanges.
- It's important to research and analyze REITs, considering factors such as the quality of the properties in their portfolio, the track record of the management team, dividend history, expense ratios, and overall market conditions.

3. Real Estate Partnerships:
- Real estate partnerships involve pooling resources with other investors to collectively invest in real estate properties.

- This can take the form of joint ventures, limited liability companies (LLCs), or partnerships.

- Real estate partnerships provide opportunities to invest in larger properties or projects that may be beyond an individual investor's reach.

- It's crucial to thoroughly evaluate the partnership structure, legal agreements, and the reputation and track record of the partners or sponsors involved.

4. Real Estate Crowdfunding:

- Real estate crowdfunding platforms allow individuals to invest in real estate projects alongside other investors.

- These platforms connect investors with real estate developers or operators seeking funding for their projects.

- Investors can choose specific projects or invest in diversified real estate portfolios offered by the platform.

- Real estate crowdfunding provides accessibility to real estate investments with lower capital requirements compared to traditional property purchases.

- Due diligence on the crowdfunding platform, project sponsor, investment terms, and the specific real estate project is essential before committing funds.

5. House Hacking:

- House hacking involves living in a property while renting out a portion of it to generate rental income.

- This strategy can be implemented in various ways, such as renting out a spare bedroom, a basement apartment, or purchasing a multi-unit property and living in one unit while renting out the others.

- House hacking can help offset or eliminate housing expenses and accelerate savings or investment potential.

When considering real estate investments, factors such as location, market conditions, cash flow projections, financing options, property management requirements, and risk tolerance should be carefully evaluated. It's also advisable to consult with real estate professionals, financial advisors, or attorneys who specialize in real estate to ensure informed decision-making and compliance with local regulations.

Creating Digital Assets and Online Businesses
Creating digital assets and online businesses can be a rewarding way to generate passive income and build a scalable business. Here's an overview of the process:

1. Choose a Niche or Product:
   - Identify a niche or product that aligns with your interests, skills, and market demand.
   - Research your target audience, competition, and potential profitability of the chosen niche.

2. Develop a Digital Asset:

- Create a digital asset, such as an e-book, online course, software application, stock photos, music, or video content.
- Ensure that your digital asset provides value to your target audience and stands out from competitors.

3. Build an Online Presence:
- Establish a professional website or blog to showcase your digital asset and provide information to potential customers.
- Optimize your online presence for search engines (SEO) to increase visibility and attract organic traffic.
- Utilize social media platforms, email marketing, and content marketing strategies to build an audience and promote your digital asset.

4. Monetization Strategies:
- Determine how you will monetize your digital asset. Some common strategies include:
  - Selling the asset directly: Offer your digital asset for sale on your website or through online marketplaces.

- Subscription or membership model: Charge a recurring fee for access to your digital content or services.

- Licensing or royalties: Allow others to use your digital asset in exchange for licensing fees or royalties.

- Affiliate marketing: Promote relevant products or services through affiliate links and earn commissions for referred sales.

5. E-commerce and Online Stores:

- If you plan to sell physical products online, consider setting up an e-commerce store.

- Choose a suitable platform, optimize product listings, provide secure payment options, and focus on customer service.

6. Advertising and Sponsorships:

- Generate revenue through online advertising by partnering with ad networks or displaying targeted ads on your website or blog.

- Seek sponsorships from relevant brands or companies that align with your niche and audience.

7. Automate Processes and Scale:
- Automate repetitive tasks by utilizing tools and software to streamline operations and save time.
- As your online business grows, consider outsourcing certain tasks or hiring virtual assistants to manage day-to-day operations.

8. Continual Improvement and Adaptation:
- Monitor your website analytics, sales data, customer feedback, and market trends to identify areas for improvement and adapt your strategies accordingly.
- Stay updated with industry developments, emerging technologies, and changing customer preferences to stay ahead of the competition.

Remember that building a successful online business and generating passive income requires dedication, persistence, and ongoing learning. Keep refining your strategies, engaging with your audience, and delivering value to maintain and grow your digital assets and online presence.

Chapter 6

Navigating the Tax Landscape

Navigating the tax landscape is an important aspect of managing your finances and investments. Here are some key considerations when it comes to taxes:

1. Understand Tax Laws and Regulations:
 - Stay informed about tax laws and regulations that are relevant to your income sources, investments, and business activities.
 - Regularly review updates from tax authorities and consult with tax professionals or advisors to ensure compliance.

2. Keep Accurate Records:
- Maintain organized and accurate records of your income, expenses, and investments.
- Retain supporting documentation, such as receipts, invoices, bank statements, and investment statements, to substantiate your tax deductions and transactions.

3. Determine Your Tax Filing Status:
- Understand the criteria for different tax filing statuses, such as single, married filing jointly, married filing separately, or head of household.
- Choose the status that provides the most favorable tax treatment based on your situation.

4. Report All Income:
- Ensure that you report all sources of income, including salary, wages, rental income, interest, dividends, capital gains, and any other taxable income.
- Familiarize yourself with the different tax forms (e.g., W-2, 1099, Schedule C) and their

requirements for reporting specific types of income.

5. Take Advantage of Deductions and Credits:
   - Identify tax deductions and credits that you are eligible for and ensure you claim them.
   - Common deductions include mortgage interest, state and local taxes, charitable contributions, student loan interest, and business expenses.
   - Research tax credits available to you, such as the Earned Income Tax Credit (EITC), Child Tax Credit, or education-related credits.

6. Capital Gains and Losses:
   - Understand the tax implications of capital gains and losses from your investments.
   - Depending on the holding period, gains or losses from the sale of stocks, bonds, real estate, or other assets may be classified as short-term or long-term capital gains.
   - Consider strategies like tax-loss harvesting to offset capital gains with capital losses and potentially reduce your overall tax liability.

7. Retirement Contributions:
   - Take advantage of tax-advantaged retirement accounts, such as 401(k)s, IRAs, or SEP-IRAs.
   - Contributions to these accounts may provide immediate tax benefits (e.g., deductions or tax-free growth) or tax advantages upon withdrawal in retirement.

8. Estimated Taxes and Withholding:
   - If you have income that is not subject to withholding (e.g., self-employment income, rental income), you may need to make estimated tax payments quarterly to avoid penalties.
   - Review your withholding allowances on Form W-4 to ensure appropriate tax withholding from your regular salary or wages.

9. Seek Professional Guidance:
   - Tax laws can be complex, and it's advisable to seek professional tax guidance from certified public accountants (CPAs) or tax advisors.

- They can provide personalized advice based on your specific situation, help you optimize your tax strategy, and ensure compliance with tax regulations.

10. Stay Updated:
   - Keep yourself informed about changes in tax laws, including new deductions, credits, or filing requirements.
   - Subscribe to reputable tax resources, follow official tax authority websites, and consult professionals to stay up-to-date with tax-related matters.

Remember that tax laws can vary depending on your country or jurisdiction, so it's important to understand the specific tax regulations applicable to your situation. Consult with tax professionals to ensure that you are properly navigating the tax landscape and optimizing your tax strategy within legal boundaries.

Understanding Tax Basics and Strategies

Understanding tax basics and implementing effective tax strategies can help you optimize your financial situation. Here's a guide to tax basics and some strategies to consider:

1. Tax Basics:

Taxable Income: Tax is generally calculated based on your taxable income, which is the amount left after subtracting deductions and exemptions from your total income.

Marginal Tax Brackets: Tax rates are progressive, meaning different portions of your income are taxed at different rates. Marginal tax brackets determine the tax rate applied to each income bracket.

Deductions: Deductions reduce your taxable income. Common deductions include mortgage interest, state and local taxes, charitable contributions, and certain business expenses.

Exemptions: Exemptions are deductions allowed for yourself, your spouse, and eligible dependents. However, exemptions have been phased out or eliminated in some tax systems.

Credits: Tax credits directly reduce your tax liability. Examples include the Child Tax Credit, Earned Income Tax Credit, and education-related credits.

Filing Status: Your filing status (e.g., single, married filing jointly, head of household) affects your tax rates, deductions, and eligibility for certain credits.

Tax Forms: Familiarize yourself with the tax forms required for reporting your income and deductions, such as W-2s, 1099s, Schedule C (for self-employment income), or Schedule A (for itemized deductions).

Tax Deadlines: Know the tax filing deadlines to avoid penalties or interest charges. In the United States, the deadline for most individuals is April 15th, unless an extension is filed.

2. Tax Strategies:

Maximize Retirement Contributions: Contribute to tax-advantaged retirement accounts like 401(k)s or IRAs to reduce your taxable income and enjoy potential tax-free growth or tax deductions.

Take Advantage of Tax-Advantaged Accounts: Utilize health savings accounts (HSAs) or flexible spending accounts (FSAs) to pay for qualified medical expenses with pre-tax dollars.

Harvest Capital Losses: Offset capital gains by selling investments that have declined in value. Capital losses can be used to offset capital gains and potentially reduce your overall tax liability.

Consider Tax-Efficient Investments: Opt for investments that generate tax-efficient returns, such as index funds or tax-managed mutual funds that minimize taxable distributions.

Charitable Giving: Donate to eligible charities to receive deductions for your contributions. Consider donating appreciated assets, as you may avoid capital gains tax on the appreciation.

Tax-Loss Harvesting: Strategically sell investments with capital losses to offset capital gains and potentially reduce your tax liability. Be mindful of wash sale rules that disallow losses if you buy back substantially identical securities within a specified period.

Use Tax-Advantaged Education Savings Plans: Contribute to 529 plans or Education

Savings Accounts (ESAs) to save for education expenses while enjoying potential tax benefits.

Consider Tax-Deferred Exchanges: Utilize tax-deferred exchanges, such as 1031 exchanges (in the U.S.), to defer taxes on the sale of certain properties by reinvesting the proceeds into like-kind properties.

Plan for Qualified Dividends and Long-Term Capital Gains: Long-term capital gains and qualified dividends are generally taxed at lower rates than ordinary income. Consider holding investments for longer periods to take advantage of these favorable rates.

Coordinate Spousal Income: If you're married, consider optimizing your tax situation by balancing income between spouses to potentially lower your overall tax liability.

These strategies are general considerations, and their applicability depends on your specific circumstances and the tax laws of your jurisdiction. Consult with

Maximizing Deductions and Tax Efficiency

Maximizing deductions and improving tax efficiency can help reduce your taxable income and optimize your overall tax situation. Here are some strategies to consider:

1. Itemize Deductions vs. Standard Deduction:
   - Evaluate whether itemizing deductions or taking the standard deduction is more beneficial for you. Itemizing deductions allows you to claim eligible expenses, such as mortgage interest, state and local taxes, medical expenses,

and charitable contributions, that exceed the standard deduction amount.

2. Maximize Retirement Contributions:
   - Contribute the maximum amount allowed to tax-advantaged retirement accounts such as 401(k)s, IRAs, or self-employed retirement plans. These contributions can lower your taxable income in the year they are made, potentially reducing your overall tax liability.

3. Health Savings Accounts (HSAs):
   - Contribute to an HSA if you have a high-deductible health plan. HSA contributions are tax-deductible, and withdrawals used for qualified medical expenses are tax-free. Unused funds can be carried forward and invested for future use.

4. Flexible Spending Accounts (FSAs):
   - Take advantage of FSAs offered by employers to set aside pre-tax dollars for qualified medical expenses or dependent care expenses. Ensure you estimate your expenses

accurately, as unused funds may be forfeited at the end of the plan year.

5. Deductible Business Expenses:
   - If you have a business or are self-employed, maximize your deductions by keeping track of eligible business expenses such as office supplies, equipment, travel expenses, professional fees, and home office expenses. Consult with a tax professional to ensure compliance with the rules and regulations.

6. Education-Related Tax Benefits:
   - Explore education-related tax credits and deductions, such as the American Opportunity Credit or the Lifetime Learning Credit, which can help offset qualified education expenses for yourself, your spouse, or your dependents.

7. Rental Property Deductions:
   - If you own rental properties, take advantage of deductions such as mortgage interest, property taxes, insurance, repairs, maintenance costs, and depreciation. Consult with a tax professional

who specializes in real estate to ensure you are maximizing your deductions.

8. Timing of Income and Expenses:
   - Consider the timing of income and expenses to optimize your tax situation. For example, if you anticipate a higher income in the current year, you may want to defer income to the following year or accelerate deductions into the current year.

9. Tax-Efficient Investments:
   - Consider tax-efficient investment strategies, such as investing in index funds or tax-managed mutual funds that minimize taxable distributions. These investments can help reduce the tax impact on your investment returns.

10. Consult with a Tax Professional:
   - Engage the services of a qualified tax professional or CPA who can provide personalized advice based on your specific financial situation. They can help identify

additional deductions, tax credits, or strategies that are applicable to your circumstances.

Remember to keep detailed records and documentation to support your deductions and claims. Tax laws and regulations can be complex, so consulting with a tax professional is highly recommended to ensure compliance and optimize your tax efficiency within the legal boundaries.

Planning for Retirement and Tax-Advantaged Accounts

Planning for retirement involves setting goals, estimating expenses, and selecting the right tax-advantaged accounts to save and invest for your future. Here are some key considerations:

1. Determine Your Retirement Goals:
   - Start by envisioning your ideal retirement lifestyle and estimating the expenses associated with it. Consider factors such as housing,

healthcare, travel, hobbies, and any other financial commitments.

2. Calculate Retirement Savings Needs:

- Assess how much money you'll need to accumulate by the time you retire. Consider factors like inflation, life expectancy, and potential healthcare costs. Online retirement calculators can help you estimate your savings target.

3. Understand Tax-Advantaged Retirement Accounts:

- Familiarize yourself with tax-advantaged retirement accounts available in your country, such as 401(k)s, IRAs, Roth IRAs, SEP-IRAs (for self-employed individuals), or pension plans. Each account has different tax benefits and contribution limits.

4. Contribute to Employer-Sponsored Plans:

- If your employer offers a retirement plan like a 401(k) or 403(b), contribute at least enough to receive the maximum employer match.

Employer matching is essentially free money that boosts your retirement savings.

5. Individual Retirement Accounts (IRAs):
   - Consider contributing to a Traditional IRA or Roth IRA, depending on your eligibility and circumstances. Traditional IRAs offer tax deductions on contributions, while Roth IRAs provide tax-free withdrawals in retirement.

6. Take Advantage of Catch-Up Contributions:
   - If you're 50 years or older, you may be eligible for catch-up contributions to retirement accounts. These allow you to contribute additional funds beyond the regular contribution limits, helping you accelerate your savings.

7. Diversify Your Retirement Portfolio:
   - Allocate your retirement savings across a diversified portfolio of investments, such as stocks, bonds, mutual funds, or exchange-traded

funds (ETFs). Diversification can help manage risk and potentially increase returns.

8. Manage Retirement Account Investments:
   - Regularly review and adjust your investment strategy within your retirement accounts. Consider factors like your risk tolerance, time horizon, and market conditions. You may choose to rebalance periodically to maintain your desired asset allocation.

9. Minimize Early Withdrawals and Penalties:
   - Be mindful of early withdrawal penalties and taxes associated with taking money out of retirement accounts before reaching the eligible age. Plan your finances to avoid unnecessary withdrawals that may erode your savings.

10. Plan for Required Minimum Distributions (RMDs):

- Understand the rules regarding required minimum distributions (RMDs) from retirement accounts, typically starting at age 72 (in the United States). Failing to take RMDs can result in significant penalties, so plan ahead to meet these requirements.

11. Seek Professional Guidance:
  - Consider consulting with a financial advisor or retirement specialist who can provide personalized advice based on your goals, financial situation, and risk tolerance. They can help you develop a comprehensive retirement plan and investment strategy.

Remember that retirement planning is a long-term process, and regular review and adjustments are necessary to stay on track. Start saving and investing as early as possible to take advantage of compounding growth. A solid retirement plan combined with tax-advantaged accounts can significantly enhance your ability to achieve your retirement goals.

Chapter 7

Protecting and Preserving Your Wealth

Protecting and preserving your wealth is crucial for long-term financial security. Here are some key strategies to consider:

1. Risk Management and Insurance:
   - Assess your insurance needs and ensure you have appropriate coverage for your assets, health, life, disability, and liability. Insurance can help protect against unexpected events that could negatively impact your wealth.

2. Estate Planning:
   - Create or update your estate plan, including a will, trust, and power of attorney. Consider working with an estate planning attorney to ensure your assets are distributed according to your wishes and to minimize estate taxes.

3. Asset Allocation and Diversification:
   - Maintain a diversified investment portfolio that aligns with your risk tolerance and financial

goals. Diversification across asset classes, such as stocks, bonds, real estate, and alternative investments, can help reduce risk and preserve wealth.

4. Regular Portfolio Review:
   - Conduct periodic reviews of your investment portfolio to assess its performance and make adjustments as needed. Consider rebalancing your portfolio to maintain your desired asset allocation and risk level.

5. Emergency Fund:
   - Maintain an emergency fund with three to six months' worth of living expenses. This fund serves as a financial safety net and can help protect your wealth during unexpected events or financial setbacks.

6. Long-Term Care Planning:
   - Consider long-term care insurance or other strategies to cover potential future healthcare needs. Long-term care costs can be significant

and may erode your wealth if not properly planned for.

7. Tax Efficiency:
   - Optimize your tax strategy by taking advantage of tax-efficient investments, utilizing tax-advantaged accounts, and employing tax planning strategies. Minimizing taxes can help preserve your wealth and increase its growth over time.

8. Regular Financial Checkups:
   - Conduct regular financial checkups to review your financial goals, track your progress, and make necessary adjustments. This includes monitoring your spending, savings, and investment performance.

9. Continual Education and Financial Literacy:
   - Stay informed about personal finance, investment strategies, and wealth management. Continually educate yourself to make informed

decisions and adapt to changing financial landscapes.

10. Professional Advice:
   - Consider working with a financial advisor or wealth manager who can provide personalized guidance and expertise in managing and preserving your wealth. They can help create a comprehensive wealth management plan tailored to your specific goals and circumstances.

11. Minimize Debt and Manage Liabilities:
   - Aim to minimize high-interest debt and manage liabilities responsibly. Paying off debts can free up resources and reduce financial stress, allowing you to preserve and grow your wealth more effectively.

12. Maintain Strong Cybersecurity:
   - Protect your wealth from cyber threats by practicing good cybersecurity habits. Use secure passwords, enable two-factor authentication, regularly update your software, and be cautious

of phishing attempts and suspicious online activities.

Remember that preserving and protecting your wealth requires ongoing diligence, proactive planning, and adaptability. Regularly reassess your financial situation, adjust your strategies as needed, and seek professional advice when necessary. By implementing these strategies, you can work towards safeguarding your wealth for yourself and future generations.

Estate Planning and Asset Protection

Estate planning and asset protection are essential components of wealth management. They involve strategies to ensure the orderly distribution of assets, minimize estate taxes, and protect your wealth from potential risks. Here are key considerations:

1. Will and Trust:

- Create a will that specifies how you want your assets to be distributed upon your death. Consider setting up a trust, such as a revocable living trust or an irrevocable trust, which can provide more control, privacy, and flexibility in estate planning.

2. Power of Attorney and Healthcare Proxy:
- Designate a trusted individual to act on your behalf for financial and healthcare decisions if you become incapacitated. Establishing a power of attorney and healthcare proxy ensures that your interests are protected and your wishes are followed.

3. Estate Tax Planning:
- Understand the estate tax laws in your jurisdiction and work with an estate planning attorney to implement strategies to minimize estate taxes. This may involve techniques such as gifting, establishing a family limited partnership, or utilizing estate tax exemptions and deductions.

4. Beneficiary Designations:
 - Review and update beneficiary designations on your retirement accounts, life insurance policies, and other assets. Ensure they align with your current wishes to avoid potential conflicts or unintended consequences.

5. Asset Titling:
 - Consider the appropriate titling of your assets to maximize protection and minimize probate. This may include joint tenancy with rights of survivorship, tenancy by the entirety, or using a transfer-on-death (TOD) or payable-on-death (POD) designation.

6. Asset Protection Strategies:
 - Protect your assets from potential risks, such as lawsuits or creditor claims. Strategies may include utilizing trusts, limited liability companies (LLCs), or incorporating assets into retirement accounts or insurance policies with asset protection features.

7. Charitable Giving:
   - Explore charitable giving strategies, such as establishing charitable trusts or donor-advised funds, to support causes you care about while potentially reducing estate taxes.

8. Long-Term Care Planning:
   - Plan for potential long-term care needs, such as nursing home or in-home care, by considering long-term care insurance or other funding options. This can help protect your assets from being depleted due to healthcare expenses.

9. Regular Estate Plan Review:
   - Conduct periodic reviews of your estate plan to ensure it reflects your current wishes, accounts for any changes in your financial situation or family circumstances, and remains aligned with applicable laws and regulations.

10. Seek Professional Guidance:

- Work with an experienced estate planning attorney and other professionals, such as financial advisors and tax professionals, to develop a comprehensive estate plan and asset protection strategy tailored to your specific needs and objectives.

Remember that estate planning and asset protection are complex areas, and the strategies may vary depending on your jurisdiction and individual circumstances. It's important to seek professional advice to ensure your estate plan is legally sound and addresses your specific goals and concerns.

Insurance Essentials for Financial Security

Insurance plays a crucial role in providing financial security and protecting against unforeseen events. Here are some insurance essentials to consider:

1. Health Insurance:

- Health insurance covers medical expenses and helps protect you from high healthcare costs. It provides access to medical services, prescription medications, preventive care, and emergency treatment. Choose a plan that suits your needs and consider factors such as premiums, deductibles, co-pays, and network coverage.

2. Life Insurance:

- Life insurance provides financial protection for your loved ones in the event of your death. It pays out a lump sum or regular income to your beneficiaries, helping them cover expenses such as mortgage payments, education costs, and everyday living expenses. Evaluate your coverage needs based on your financial obligations and the well-being of your dependents.

3. Disability Insurance:

- Disability insurance provides income replacement if you become unable to work due to a disability or illness. It ensures that you can meet your financial obligations and maintain your standard of living. Consider both short-term and long-term disability insurance, as they offer different coverage periods and benefits.

4. Auto Insurance:

   - Auto insurance protects against financial loss due to accidents, theft, or damage to your vehicle. It also provides liability coverage for injuries or property damage you may cause to others. Ensure that your policy meets the minimum legal requirements and consider additional coverage options such as comprehensive and collision insurance.

5. Homeowners/Renters Insurance:

   - Homeowners insurance protects your home and its contents against perils such as fire, theft, or natural disasters. It also provides liability coverage in case someone is injured on your property. Renters insurance covers personal belongings and liability in a rented property. Review your policy to ensure it adequately covers your property and possessions.

6. Umbrella Insurance:
   - Umbrella insurance provides additional liability coverage beyond the limits of your other insurance policies. It helps protect your assets in the event of a lawsuit or substantial claim. Consider umbrella insurance if you have significant assets or face a higher risk of liability.

7. Long-Term Care Insurance:
   - Long-term care insurance covers the costs associated with long-term care services, such as nursing homes, assisted living, or in-home care. It helps protect your assets and provides financial assistance for potential long-term care needs. Evaluate this insurance based on your age, health, family history, and financial circumstances.

8. Business Insurance:
   - If you own a business, consider business insurance to protect against risks such as property damage, liability claims, or business

interruption. Common types of business insurance include general liability, professional liability (errors and omissions), property insurance, and workers' compensation.

9. Travel Insurance:
   - Travel insurance provides coverage for unexpected events while traveling, such as trip cancellation, medical emergencies, lost baggage, or travel delays. Evaluate the coverage and exclusions carefully, especially for international travel or high-risk activities.

10. Regular Insurance Reviews:
   - Regularly review your insurance policies to ensure they adequately cover your needs and circumstances. As life changes, update your coverage accordingly, such as after major life events, changes in assets, or career transitions.

Remember to compare insurance options, review policy terms and conditions, and understand the coverage limits and deductibles. Work with reputable insurance providers and consider seeking guidance from an insurance professional or broker to ensure you have the appropriate coverage for your specific needs.

Long-Term Care and Retirement Planning
Long-term care (LTC) and retirement planning are closely linked as they both involve preparing for future financial needs. Here are key considerations when it comes to long-term care and retirement planning:

1. Understand Long-Term Care:
   - Educate yourself about long-term care, which refers to a range of services and support needed when an individual has difficulty performing daily activities independently. This may include assistance with bathing, dressing, eating, and mobility. Long-term care can be provided at home, in assisted living facilities, or nursing homes.

2. Assess Long-Term Care Needs:

- Evaluate your potential long-term care needs based on factors such as family medical history, personal health, lifestyle, and current support network. Consider the likelihood of needing long-term care services and the associated costs.

3. Long-Term Care Insurance:
- Explore long-term care insurance as a way to help cover the costs of future long-term care services. Long-term care insurance policies typically pay for a portion of in-home care, assisted living, or nursing home expenses. Research various policies, coverage options, elimination periods, benefit amounts, and inflation protection riders.

4. Self-Funding:
- Consider self-funding your long-term care needs by setting aside savings specifically designated for potential future care expenses. This may involve building a separate investment portfolio or earmarking a portion of your retirement savings for long-term care purposes.

5. Retirement Savings and Investments:

  - Prioritize building a robust retirement savings portfolio to provide a financial cushion for both retirement and potential long-term care needs. Maximize contributions to tax-advantaged retirement accounts like 401(k)s, IRAs, or Roth IRAs. Invest wisely to grow your savings over time.

6. Health Savings Accounts (HSAs):

  - If eligible, contribute to an HSA, which allows you to save money for medical expenses in retirement. HSAs offer tax advantages, and unused funds can be used to cover long-term care costs in the future.

7. Social Security and Medicare:

  - Understand the role of Social Security and Medicare in retirement and long-term care planning. Be aware of the age at which you become eligible for benefits and consider the impact of timing on your financial situation. Familiarize yourself with Medicare coverage and potential gaps in long-term care expenses.

8. Create a Retirement Budget:

- Develop a retirement budget that accounts for potential long-term care costs. Consider including a separate category for long-term care expenses and incorporate them into your overall retirement planning.

9. Continual Monitoring and Adjustments:

- Regularly review and reassess your long-term care and retirement plans. Keep track of changes in your health, lifestyle, and financial situation. Stay informed about evolving long-term care options and potential funding sources.

10. Seek Professional Guidance:

- Consider consulting with a financial advisor or long-term care specialist who can provide personalized advice based on your unique circumstances. They can help you evaluate options, estimate costs, and develop a comprehensive long-term care and retirement plan.

Remember that long-term care costs can be substantial and have the potential to impact your retirement savings significantly. By planning ahead and considering the various financial options available, you can better prepare for the potential costs of long-term care while safeguarding your retirement goals and financial security.

Chapter 8

Embracing a Wealth Conscious Lifestyle

Embracing a wealth-conscious lifestyle involves adopting a mindset and making intentional choices that support your financial well-being and long-term wealth creation. Here are some key principles to consider:

1. Financial Awareness:

- Stay informed about your financial situation by tracking income, expenses, and investments. Regularly review your financial goals, budgets, and progress towards achieving them. Being aware of your financial standing enables you to make informed decisions.

2. Goal Setting:

- Define clear and measurable financial goals that align with your values and aspirations. Whether it's saving for retirement, buying a home, starting a business, or achieving financial independence, setting goals provides a roadmap for your wealth journey.

3. Budgeting and Spending Discipline:
   - Create a budget to track and manage your income and expenses. Prioritize your spending based on your goals and values, distinguishing between needs and wants. Cultivate discipline in your spending habits and avoid unnecessary debt.

4. Saving and Investing:
   - Cultivate a habit of saving and consistently allocate a portion of your income towards savings and investments. Establish an emergency fund to cover unexpected expenses and invest in diversified assets such as stocks, bonds, real estate, or mutual funds to grow your wealth over time.

5. Continuous Learning:
   - Commit to ongoing financial education and self-improvement. Stay updated on investment strategies, personal finance, tax laws, and

economic trends. Expand your knowledge through books, podcasts, seminars, and seeking advice from trusted financial professionals.

6. Mindful Consumption:
   - Practice mindful consumption by being intentional about your purchases. Avoid impulsive spending and consider the value and utility of the items you buy. Prioritize quality over quantity and seek experiences and investments that provide long-term value.

7. Debt Management:
   - Minimize and manage debt responsibly. Differentiate between good debt (such as a mortgage for a home or student loans for education) and bad debt (such as high-interest credit card debt). Pay off high-interest debt as soon as possible and use debt strategically to build wealth.

8. Surround Yourself with Like-Minded Individuals:

- Seek out a supportive network of individuals who share similar financial goals and values. Engage in conversations about wealth creation, share knowledge and experiences, and learn from each other's successes and challenges.

9. Charitable Giving:
   - Incorporate philanthropy into your financial plan. Support causes you care about by donating time, money, or resources. Giving back not only benefits others but also cultivates gratitude and a sense of purpose.

10. Regular Financial Checkups:
   - Schedule regular financial checkups to assess your progress, review your goals, and adjust your strategies if necessary. This allows you to stay on track, make necessary course corrections, and stay aligned with your wealth-conscious lifestyle.

Remember that embracing a wealth-conscious lifestyle is a long-term commitment and requires discipline, patience, and perseverance. By adopting these principles and making conscious choices, you can cultivate financial well-being, build wealth, and ultimately achieve your financial goals.

Balancing Lifestyle Choices with Financial Goals

Balancing lifestyle choices with financial goals is an important aspect of achieving overall financial well-being. It involves making conscious decisions about how you allocate your resources and prioritize your spending. Here are some tips for finding a balance:

1. Define Your Priorities:
   - Clarify your financial goals and identify your core values. Determine what matters most to you in terms of your lifestyle choices. This will help you make decisions that align with your priorities.

2. Create a Realistic Budget:

- Develop a budget that reflects both your financial goals and your desired lifestyle. Allocate funds for essential expenses, savings, debt payments, and discretionary spending. Be realistic about what you can afford and adjust your budget as needed.

3. Track Your Expenses:
   - Keep track of your spending to gain a clear understanding of where your money goes. Use budgeting tools or apps to monitor your expenses and identify areas where you may be overspending or where you can cut back.

4. Differentiate Between Needs and Wants:
   - Distinguish between essential needs and discretionary wants. Focus on meeting your needs first, such as housing, food, healthcare, and debt obligations. Evaluate your wants and consider whether they align with your financial goals.

5. Set Boundaries:

- Establish boundaries and guidelines for your spending. Determine what is reasonable and sustainable for your financial situation. This may involve setting spending limits for certain categories or implementing a "wait-and-reflect" period for larger purchases.

6. Seek Value and Balance:
- Strive for value-driven spending by seeking experiences and purchases that align with your values and provide long-term satisfaction. Look for opportunities to enjoy life without compromising your financial goals. Find a balance between enjoying the present and planning for the future.

7. Find Creative Alternatives:
- Explore cost-effective alternatives that allow you to enjoy your desired lifestyle without overspending. Look for free or low-cost activities, utilize discounts or coupons, consider do-it-yourself (DIY) projects, and seek out affordable ways to achieve your desired experiences.

8. Continual Evaluation and Adjustment:
   - Regularly review your financial situation, goals, and lifestyle choices. Assess whether your spending aligns with your priorities and make adjustments as needed. Be open to modifying your choices as circumstances change or new opportunities arise.

9. Seek Professional Advice:
   - Consider consulting with a financial advisor who can help you develop a personalized financial plan that balances your lifestyle choices with your financial goals. They can provide guidance and strategies to help you find the right balance.

10. Practice Self-discipline and Delayed Gratification:
   - Cultivate self-discipline and the ability to delay gratification. Understand that making short-term sacrifices or choosing less

extravagant options can contribute to long-term financial success. Stay focused on your goals and remind yourself of the bigger picture.

Remember that finding a balance between lifestyle choices and financial goals is a personal journey. It requires self-awareness, discipline, and ongoing evaluation. By being intentional and mindful about your choices, you can strike a balance that allows you to enjoy your life while working towards financial stability and long-term success.

Building Healthy Financial Habits
Building healthy financial habits is crucial for achieving financial stability and long-term success. Here are some key habits to help you build a solid financial foundation:

1. Create a Budget:
   - Establish a budget that outlines your income, expenses, and savings goals. Track your spending and ensure that you live within your

means. A budget provides a clear roadmap for managing your finances effectively.

2. Save Regularly:
 - Make saving a priority by setting aside a portion of your income each month. Aim to build an emergency fund that covers 3-6 months of living expenses. Additionally, save for specific goals such as retirement, a down payment on a home, or a dream vacation.

3. Pay Yourself First:
 - Practice the habit of paying yourself first by automating your savings. Set up automatic transfers to your savings or investment accounts before allocating funds for other expenses. This ensures that you prioritize saving and investing from the start.

4. Control Debt:
 - Minimize and manage debt responsibly. Avoid unnecessary debt and pay off high-interest debt as quickly as possible. Develop a plan to pay down outstanding balances, whether through

the debt avalanche method (prioritizing high-interest debt) or the debt snowball method (prioritizing small debts first).

5. Track Your Spending:
   - Monitor your spending habits to identify areas where you can cut back or make adjustments. Use budgeting apps or spreadsheets to categorize expenses and gain insights into your spending patterns. This helps you make informed decisions about where to allocate your resources.

6. Practice Mindful Spending:
   - Cultivate mindfulness in your spending habits. Before making a purchase, ask yourself if it aligns with your financial goals and if it brings long-term value. Differentiate between needs and wants, and consider alternatives or more cost-effective options.

7. Invest for the Future:
   - Begin investing early to take advantage of compounding growth. Explore different

investment options such as stocks, bonds, mutual funds, or real estate, based on your risk tolerance and long-term financial goals. Consider consulting with a financial advisor to develop an investment strategy.

8. Continual Learning:
   - Educate yourself about personal finance and investment strategies. Read books, follow reputable financial blogs or podcasts, and stay informed about market trends. Increasing your financial literacy empowers you to make informed decisions and adapt to changing circumstances.

9. Review and Adjust:
   - Regularly review your financial situation and make necessary adjustments. Revisit your budget, savings goals, and investment strategies to ensure they align with your evolving needs and priorities. Stay proactive in managing your finances.

10. Seek Professional Guidance:

- Consider working with a financial advisor who can provide personalized guidance based on your specific circumstances and goals. They can offer expert advice, help you develop a comprehensive financial plan, and hold you accountable to your objectives.

Remember, building healthy financial habits takes time and commitment. Be patient with yourself and focus on making consistent progress. Celebrate small wins along the way, and remain dedicated to your long-term financial well-being.

Giving Back: The Power of Philanthropy
Philanthropy, or the act of giving back to society, has the power to make a positive impact on individuals, communities, and the world as a whole. Here are some key aspects highlighting the power of philanthropy:

1. Social Impact:

- Philanthropy has the potential to address social challenges and improve the lives of others. Through charitable donations, individuals and organizations can support causes such as education, healthcare, poverty alleviation, environmental conservation, and more. Philanthropic initiatives can create lasting change and contribute to the betterment of society.

2. Empowerment and Equality:
- Philanthropy can empower marginalized communities and promote equality. By supporting initiatives that focus on social justice, access to education, gender equality, and economic empowerment, philanthropists can help create a more inclusive and fair society.

3. Addressing Critical Needs:
- Philanthropy plays a crucial role in addressing urgent and critical needs. During times of natural disasters, humanitarian crises, or other emergencies, philanthropic efforts can provide immediate relief, aid, and support to

affected communities. This rapid response can save lives and help rebuild affected areas.

4. Innovative Solutions:
   - Philanthropy can foster innovation by supporting research, development, and entrepreneurship. By funding scientific advancements, technological innovations, and social enterprises, philanthropists can drive progress and create solutions to complex societal challenges.

5. Collaborative Approaches:
   - Philanthropy encourages collaboration among individuals, organizations, and governments. By working together, philanthropists can leverage their resources, expertise, and networks to amplify their impact. Partnerships can lead to greater efficiency, effectiveness, and sustainability in addressing social issues.

6. Personal Fulfillment:

- Engaging in philanthropy can bring a sense of personal fulfillment and purpose. Giving back allows individuals to connect with their values, contribute to causes they care about, and make a positive difference in the lives of others. Philanthropy can be deeply rewarding and provide a sense of meaning and joy.

7. Legacy and Generational Impact:
- Philanthropy offers an opportunity to create a lasting legacy and impact future generations. By establishing foundations, endowments, or charitable trusts, individuals can ensure that their philanthropic efforts continue beyond their lifetime. This allows for sustained support for causes and organizations that align with their values.

8. Inspiring Others:
- Philanthropy has a ripple effect and can inspire others to give back. When individuals witness the positive impact of philanthropy, they may be inspired to engage in their own acts of

giving, creating a culture of generosity and social responsibility.

9. Corporate Social Responsibility:
 - Philanthropy is an essential aspect of corporate social responsibility (CSR). Businesses can contribute to society by incorporating philanthropic initiatives into their operations. By supporting local communities, environmental sustainability, employee volunteer programs, and ethical business practices, companies can enhance their reputation and positively impact society.

10. Global Citizenship:
 - Philanthropy promotes global citizenship and a sense of interconnectedness. Individuals and organizations can support causes beyond their immediate surroundings, embracing a broader perspective and recognizing their responsibility towards the global community.

Whether through financial contributions, volunteerism, or advocacy, philanthropy has the power to create positive change. It allows individuals to actively participate in shaping a better world and leaves a lasting impact on individuals, communities, and future generations.

Conclusion

Your Journey to Financial Mastery

In conclusion, the journey to financial mastery is a personal and lifelong pursuit. It involves acquiring knowledge, developing healthy habits, and making informed decisions that align with your financial goals. Here are the key takeaways from this journey:

1. Education is key: Take the time to educate yourself about personal finance. Learn about budgeting, saving, investing, and debt management. Continuous learning is essential to stay informed about new strategies and opportunities.

2. Set clear goals: Define your financial goals and aspirations. Having specific targets provides direction and motivation on your financial journey.

3. Budget and track your finances: Create a budget to manage your income and expenses.

Regularly track your spending to ensure it aligns with your goals. Make adjustments as necessary to maintain financial discipline.

4. Build an emergency fund: Establish a safety net by building an emergency fund. This fund will provide stability and peace of mind during unexpected situations.

5. Manage debt wisely: Develop a plan to manage and pay off debt. Prioritize high-interest debt and explore different repayment strategies. Minimize new debt and use credit responsibly.

6. Save and invest: Cultivate the habit of saving and investing. Set aside a portion of your income regularly and explore different investment options based on your risk tolerance and long-term goals.

7. Seek professional advice: Consider working with a financial advisor or planner who can provide personalized guidance and help you make informed decisions.

8. Practice discipline and patience: Financial mastery requires discipline and patience. Avoid impulsive spending, stick to your financial plan, and understand that wealth building takes time.

9. Regularly review and adjust: Continually review your financial progress, reassess your goals, and make necessary adjustments along the way. Reflect on your achievements and challenges, and learn from them.

10. Embrace a wealth-conscious mindset: Adopt a mindset that prioritizes long-term wealth creation and financial well-being. Make conscious choices that align with your goals and values.

Remember, the journey to financial mastery is unique to each individual. It's important to focus on your personal goals, stay committed to continuous improvement, and adapt your strategies as needed. With perseverance, knowledge, and the right mindset, you can achieve financial mastery and create a secure and prosperous future for yourself.

www.ingramcontent.com/pod-product-compliance
Lightning Source LLC
Chambersburg PA
CBHW071509220526
45472CB00003B/964